GW01219311

ALCHEMY OF PRAISE

Wendy Kieffer

For Jonathan

(1981-2024)

CONTENTS

III

INTRODUCTION

Dear Reader,

I try to live by faith in the One who made me and redeemed me, and so you will find that many of the poems here reflect my communion with the Creator and His creation through the many ways I encounter Him.

I have chosen to arrange this collection into three parts. In the first section, the poems draw the eyes up; they are contemplations, adorations, and prayers. The second section delves into the interior space of body and soul, where revelations and transformations occur. Finally, the focus shifts outward as I engage with the various beauties and tragedies of life. Many of the poems in this section are particularly meaningful to me as I grieve the sudden loss of my brother who struggled with addiction.

Like a bouquet, you will find in these poems a variety of shapes and forms: some cultivated using classical structures, others grown wild in a confessional style. All of them have arisen from my lived experiences as I walk with God, transformed through an alchemy of praise.

With love,
Wendy

Vision Up
collage with cotton paper and archival ink, 2024

SARAH SISCO

I

Effortlessly,
Love flows from God into man,
Like a bird
Who rivers the air
Without moving her wings.

~Mechthild of Magdeburg

A GIFT

The sky cracks,
thin as an eyelash;
through the sliver
the elements slip, raining
into a bowl of flesh and bone.

Knees to earth, shapes rise
from mood and musing
and memories
bright as stained glass.
What wonders lie in molding
a dwelling to hold an offering
of dust and mist?

Here, I discover a facet of glory
I didn't know until I made a setting
for the sense of it; praise escapes
my mouth, and You receive the song
of Your song. Is this not love?
This dance of giving
that which has been given?

I wipe my brow and arch
my spine, spent arms sweeping
back as ribs invite the sky.
I exhale the attempt to live
as if my heart beats
for any other reason.

I raise my cupped hands
and offer You Creation's
creation: a frame I made
for You, Abba, to hold
the shiny pieces of my soul.

MORNING

You open like a hand that bears a gift,
Like a mouth about to sing, like a womb.
And yesterday is folded up in light
As dreams are born again inside the dew.

The heavy veil of night, of blinding doubt,
Has lifted with the lids of my new eyes;
I am remade in the turning, turning
To the One who softly bids me *arise*.

I come to you with open palms outstretched,
And sense the strength of earth under my feet.
As wind moves through the forest in my chest,
My gaze rests on the rise and fall of leaves.

What will I say with thirty thousand breaths?
What beauty will the silences conceive?
What music will my soul compose for you
As my heart sounds a hundred thousand beats?

Whatever comes, whatever fills my hands,
May one request meet every breath and beat:
That I would have the vision of Jesus
So I might choose to love as He loves me.

WITH YOU

I cry out to You,
and You pull me close.
The rhythm of my breathing

slows as it settles into Yours.
I rest in Your warmth;
the steady drum of Your heartbeat

strengthens mine.
My fists unclench as I release
what I cannot grasp.

You tuck a piece of my hair
behind my ear and lean in to kiss
my forehead.

"I am here," You say.
I look up to find my reflection
in the deep wells of Your eyes,

my face now soft as Yours,
the emptiness lifting
with the corners of Your smile.

WHAT KIND OF KING? [part one]

What kind of king bends to the ground
To take our filth into his hands,
And kneeling as a servant, pours
Himself for that which love commands?

What kind of king trades royal robes
For a towel, a slave's apron,
And with the hands that formed the world
Lifts worn soles into the basin?

What kind of king whose knowing eyes
Behold the one whose heart betrays
And yet still washes feet that run
To usher in our dark disgrace?

What kind of king leads the battle
In a posture of surrender?
Whose power incorruptible
Can be felt in touch so tender?

ALCHEMY OF PRAISE

WHAT KIND OF KING? [part two]

What kind of king rides a donkey
And comes without armies or swords;
Whose only power on display
Is in His eyes, His heart, His words?

"What kind of king," the people cry,
"Having command over the grave,
Could not also crush the Romans—
Blessed is He who comes to save!"

What kind of king turns inside out
Our cries for justice, for bloodshed,
And overthrows the Rome within
Each of us through His blood instead?

What kind of king rules a kingdom
Of the willing, who makes His throne
From the offering laid at His feet,
The open palms of flesh and bone?

DAY UNTO DAY

Into the void crashed waves of light
  The day You spoke to darkest night.
Father of rain, Mother of dew,
  One who spun the expanse of blue:
Teach me to read deeply the skies;
  Open my ears, baptize my eyes.

Earth turned as a thought in Your mind;
  Matter and space and time combined.
In Your hands. O, Master of spheres,
  Whose grace molds and upholds my years:
Whirl me, shape me, hand over clay;
  Night unto night, day unto day.

In all things Your glory is found;
   Wordlessly, the heavens resound.
Poet of wing, of wind, of flight,
   Who paints an arc with rain and light:
Take my vision where eagles dwell
   That I might know Your poem well.

In the silence creation sings;
   Symphonies sound in Saturn's rings.
Maker of moons that peak and hide,
   Artist of stars and planets flung wide:
Bathe me in gold, clothe me in light;
   Let my life speak to darkest night.

CHASING THE WIND

I thought I saw You in the shattered
diamonds thrown across the sea
by a sun that rises swiftly
and makes no mention of the night.
I thought I heard You in the waves
that charged the shore like cavalry
and in the silence of weightlessness
that stripped me of my cares.

I thought I felt You in the veil
of moonlight draped over our heads,
in the confidence of arms that closed
around me like a shield.
I thought I touched You when I held
the golden braid that love makes,
but it quietly unraveled
under the weight of soul.

I thought I read You in my lines;
drawing breath under those lights,
I watched the vow escape my lips
like an arrow from the bow.
It soared above affirming hands
up to the gilded heights,
and then I found it lying broken
in a box under the bed.

I thought I circled You on pages,
lighting beacons in my mind.
Was it You who strummed my skin
with truth that rippled like a wave?
Did You signal with the flicker
within the steady hearths?
Did You lean into those lamplit words
and push them through the gates?

I didn't know that I was looking
for You in the mortal fruit;
the chill of undevoted skin
burned wildly down my spine.
And the drums beat their prose
against my ears and down my throat,
but their freedom was refuted
by a blackened core.

I found You when the Earth
in all her splendor proved unfit
to yield the bread my soul desired;
the appetites consumed.
I found You when I saw my life
as You would see it too,
when Mercy sent her rivers
through my desert eyes.

GOLDEN HOUR

Every night at dusk, a gallery opened outside the window
of our fourth-floor walkup: buckets of violet, rose, and rust
would splash across the inky expanse while the crimson fire
sinking low bathed the skyline in shadow.

We would stand on the threshold between the ache of grind
and the thrill of possibility, blood pounding in our feet, hungry
for nightly exhibitions that painted the lenses of our eyes.

I'd heard the striking beauty was an effect of the pollution.
Sounded like a kind of redemption. Or perhaps the sun, too,
pushed himself harder in the city, finding the cleverest point
from which to scatter light, stretching the warm wavelengths
long as they could go until his masterpiece arrested us.

What could we sense in that liminal space, once the cement paths
to glory dimmed, before the empire ignited into its glamorous glow?
With your smile soft in the golden hour, our breathing slow and easy,
wonder would reward us with an unnamed wisdom while millions
of dreamers charged ahead.

What a surprise to find, rising above the chorus of kings and queens,
a shepherd softly humming the ancient song that drew us home
every night at dusk.

ALCHEMY OF PRAISE

REDEMPTION

Shame burns
my feet, sears
my eyes, chokes
my voice.

And then, I behold
the cross

and watch
as You take the flames
out from under me
and slowly

make a torch.

You hand it to me,
my face warm
in the radiance.

I lift it high,
a pool of light
spreading at my feet.

Vision In
collage with cotton paper and archival ink, 2024

SARAH SISCO

II

If I am peaceful, I shall see
Beauty's face continually;
Feeding on her wine and bread.

~Sara Teasdale

THE SPARK

Where does it come from—
the spark that ignites synapses
to wire commands
for sinew and bone
to harness the wind?
To make a cage of fingers
around the smallest
living things?
To write it all down?

WEIGHTLESS

Countless migratory birds cruise into the Florida sun,
weaving a whimsical canopy above as I plunge

into a cool shock of blue; I shoot through soothing resistance,
trailing roaring ripples, and dive under to find myself

surrounded by ribbons of refracted light, hundreds of rainbows
pulsing along the underwater walls. I release an endless

exhale, sending a dream of fingertips to brush playfully
over my cheeks. I turn to rest, to drift on the quiet surface;

sun soaks my boundaryless skin; the flag draws me
into its undulations; my name floats among feathers

riding soft thermal currents. I am weightless, wrapped in silk,
and burdens have no bones to carry them.

Soon I will emerge. Heavy feet will mark their temporary outlines
across the cement. Countless pixels glowing in liquid crystal

will hook the eyes and drag it all down. Skin like iron, I will burn
with infinite impulses until the flight of birds breaks into my chest,

tracing patterns on my tongue as I plunge once more into wonder.

OCEAN

Ocean, deep as memory, unsearchable as dreams,
I am stilled and opened as I listen to you breathe.

Light dances in your valleys; scores of diamonds flash.
What treasures lie in wait for their glory to be grasped?

Your beauty has no limit, expanding infinitely;
You remind me I am small, just a creature by the sea.

And yet you call me out into the bright unknown,
Where nothing can be tamed; nothing can be owned.

Here you present your gift: you say, "Child, come and play!
Be untangled from the world, toss yourself upon my waves.

"Lie back, let me carry you—feel how light you become
While resting in the sway like new life in the womb.

"When you return to shore and lay your heavy bones
On the warm chest of Earth whose arms welcome you home,

"And Sun pours his honey beneath your glistening skin
While Wind plays her music on you, her violin,

"May the whisper in the shell that seems to know your name
Show you the 'I love you' in everything that's made."

FLIGHT

I love the way water resists
the force of gravity.
Here, nothing heavy exists.
Even the tread of thoughts marching
around the edges of my mind
is casually erased by the current.
Plans dissolve, slipping into the swirl
of the eddy, and the day's momentum
is soft and smooth as soaring.

When my body is buoyant, I am free
to move as if through dreams.

So I often seek ablution in this river;
leaning back on a raft, I am nothing
more than a passenger.
The sun, my molten lava cake.
The river, my ice cream.
The wind, my imagination.
The wide arc of sky, my deepest love.

FASHIONING

Every word I speak colors my lips;
my thoughts effuse a fragrance.

I taste every image I see, feeding
desires that grow to frame my face.

Wishes flash in my smile;
questions dangle from my ears.

My dress contains beliefs;
my coat is made of prayers.

The wounds I carry hang near my heart,
catching the sun.

My skin holds that which touches me;
the one I serve is tattooed on my hand.

My stride tells of where I've been;
where I'm going lights my eyes.

And when I enter a room or a heart,
it all comes with me.

NEW GROWTH

This morning when I awoke, I came to the mirror
and saw that the shape and color of my eyes had changed.
Compassion had widened them ever so, and the wisdom
they'd been seeking had brightened the rings of green and brown
as if clouds over a field of oaks had cleared away.

My lips were softer, too, and more accustomed to laughing.
My jaw was unclenched, my shoulders content
with the load they carried. And yesterday's birdsong
was still braided into my hair.

I shall be satisfied when I awake in Your likeness.
~Psalm 17:15

LAST NIGHT OF US

We took a selfie before there was a word for it
at Mamoun's in The Village; devoured falafel
sandwiches, tahini dripping down my chin,
snow flurrying behind glass like a lifetime
of sketches had been torn to bits and tossed.

It was the night before we gave birth. Coats on,
we look giddy with cold, our smiles swallowing
up the last night of *us*.

We wept that night on the bed, holding hands;
we broke open and all that would never be
the same spilled out. I can still taste something
sweet in our sadness, a hint it would be
worth it. Somehow, we must've known
that we were falling like a grain of wheat.

SMOKE

Poets are always burning

something

on the stove.

MATRESCENCE

To the feline prowess of my former self, your ballerina back,
your lithe limbs stalking my bare reflection: I cowered at the foot

of your legacy, trembling like a golden leaf at all that had fallen
beyond my reach. I searched the slack wreck of skin that had cracked

into scars stretching the width of a doorway to accommodate not one
but two. The sales lady hung a bigger size over the door and chimed,

"See how that one feels." You crouched close as I examined eyes
underlined by black smudges and eternal vigilance: the cross

my mother wore around my neck. You circled me, your frame gliding
effortlessly while I wailed silently, the used-up puddle of skin cupped

in my hands. You'd never held a world in your arms, never fallen
into love so clear and pure, never known the gift wrapped in flames

on the altar. But there I was, bankrupt of your beauty's high currency,
emptied out in a dressing room, shaking while trying on Spanx.

"How are you doing in there?" she rang. "Fine," I managed,
but she must've known that no one who shopped there was fine.

I stretched the unyielding nylon over your melted down trophy,
compressing the mess. I waited until I was driving home to scream

like an ambulance through the streets. But there they were, waiting
at the window, beaming at the sight of my face. They love to touch

my belly, lay a cheek on their first home, squish the purply marks
like modeling clay and ask why it's so soft. I've learned to answer,

"Because it was so strong." What is a stretchmark if not a refusal to
break?
And then a day came when I realized suddenly what had happened

gradually: my needs had stretched to accommodate their breath
and song. Now here we are, spinning like a carnival ride; my oak back

and iron arms suspend them in whorls of golden laughter. Their eyes
reflect me: I am radiant, smiling with unspeakable joy, no longer moaning

like a domestic stray that doesn't know the scars across her mouth
spell *love*. And there you are, quietly, laying yourself down at my feet.

COMPELLED TO TURN

By the wind of a thousand closing doors,
to the crab spider: fishing the air, hunting
in stillness, suspended by the anticipation
of hunger—survival now depending
on the ability to do nothing.

To the blooms in the yard I've barely noticed,
whose violet tongues unfurl in time
for the cup of redemption.

To the impish breeze that lifts my hair,
tosses it over my face
and races up into the palms.

They tell us not to touch,
but I've never felt more.
It's true how losing one sense
strengthens those that remain.

Teach me stillness. Strip me down,
bare as dirt. Bathe me in pelting rain.
When I rise, let me heed the words
on the wind. Let my brow be a sea of glass.
Let my eyes stare straight into the sun
inside the dew.

And when Earth spins again,
don't let me choke on the dust
she kicks up, or let me be blinded
by the whirl.

THE PORCH THAT WRAPPED
AROUND MY PLANS

Was the only thing left standing
after it all came down.

So, we made a home there for a while.

At first, it was invigorating
(except for the persistent news of death)
to breathe outside, to huddle together,
to notice the sounds of creeping things
and the patterns of soaring things.

And I burned a little brighter,
and the earth took on that striking
edge until I started to see the potential
emerging from the dirt.
I began digging, pulling, aching,
buying, planting, returning, plotting,
searching, arching, creaking, settling.

It seems there is something about
my porch that can't help but wrap
itself around plans,

every breath the hammering of a nail.

ALCHEMY OF PRAISE

THE HUNGER

The more I listen to the sigh and groan
of wheels sailing over slick roads,
the more they sound like waves breaking
on the shore, and the train whistle's wail
like some large beast breaching the surf;
my family is asleep as I write at the window
of an imagined cabin by the sea.

I often ache for the ocean and open skies,
for the garden I've only dreamed of
somewhere near the *bee-loud glade*,
where my children run barefoot
through a meadow they've named.
With fingernails black as ink, they grow
among trees that teach them how to live
rooted and wild, tender and fierce.

Yet I'm reminded on nights like these
how beauty greens even here, emerging
from the need and hunger. Leaves grow verdant
in my mind as winter strips Queens of hers,
and the sea moaning within often lulls
and comforts me. Even when icy, callous winds
whip through the tunnels of concrete that sprawl
under a gray sliver of sky, starlight finds a way
to shatter into gold on every cell.

SLOW BURN

Sometimes I try to recall the way time felt as a child,
when being came as easy as contemplating the millipede
or the business of bees; when the only thing on the schedule
was to follow a breeze that sang of the coming rain.

I miss the freedom to burn time, to not know the guilt
of squandering it or the sting of regret when it is lost—
because I lived inside of it, and it held me like the ocean.

It seems now every minute is haunted by accomplishment;
the whisper of its finitude rides in on every gust of wind,
and being has become another task on the list.

SPIDERWEBS

The truth that I will die
hangs light as spiderwebs
above every branch,
every threshold,
every brow.

But the truth that I will rise
is strong as bedrock
and bright as noon.

Vision Out
collage with cotton paper and archival ink, 2024

SARAH SISCO

III

To stare with yearning eyes into darkness,
To extend lonely hands into space,
To turn an ear toward the rustle of leaves,
To pray for a miracle, to yearn for a sign.

~Rachel Bluwstein

THE BANQUET

We found the banquet prepared for our eyes
And with open ears, we stood and listened
For Beauty calling across years and miles.

She sang, she cried, she danced in all her styles;
And when the rooms seemed to hum and glisten,
We found the banquet prepared for our eyes.

The masters carried us into the skies
On the strokes from hands that bled precision
For Beauty calling across years and miles.

The compositions held their sacred cries,
As if death created no partition;
We found the banquet prepared for our eyes.

Filled with wonder, our praise began to rise,
As glory to the Maker was given
For Beauty calling across years and miles.

Such vision is not grounded where it lies,
But steals away inside hearts commissioned.
We found the banquet prepared for our eyes,
For Beauty calling across years and miles.

VAN GOGH

It's not the luminous pears,
green skin awash in first love,
framed in suspension of decay,
or the holy sole of a boot, dripping
with all I've ever wanted to be.
It's not the passion in sunflowers—
those stalky, wide-faced forms stroked
like a lover's hair, *gratefully*.
It's not the rage in the pupils or the burdens
hanging on the mouths.
It's not even the scintillating stars singing praise,
the roiling eruptions of light, the loneliness
of beauty or the tragedy of obscurity.

It's her eyes.

They caught me off guard. My soul still shakes,
the distance between my suffering and hers
erased.

THE TABLE

Is a field your laughter races across to find mine
rolling through the wheat beneath our crescent eyes
so full of stars; your shoulders shake, breath caught
in a quake of joy. Steam rises to meet our tears
from bread broken in bliss.

This is our song, born of a long history of fire
and cloud; grateful mouths open wide for miracles,
for sustenance, for the yield of light and water woven
through soil and seed. Steeped in the candles' amber,
night pressing against the windows, we clap and pound
the rhythms of what it means to be human.

And I see, gathered around me, the salty, the sweet,
the silly, the deep; breaking and sharing pieces of ourselves,
drinking distillations of who we are and where we've been;
you lean in, smile impish and wide, and embellish a story
that warms our bellies.

Our table is a stage, and all the parts are set until we reach
a different age, but key players are missing, and a name spoken
hangs in silence as all that he was quivers in the mind's eye.

Tonight, we sit at an altar next to holy hands that have kneaded,
mixed and measured love, folding it into every bite.
Nana's sterling presides over an offering of fire as we taste and see
that the Lord is good. And all the flavors mingling on our tongues—
the saltiness of tears, the bitterness of history, the blessings
in our glasses, eternity's lilt in our laughter—will ring in the mouths
of little ones as they tumble through the years.

The table is the edge at which we soften our own; we are light
and diaphanous as the lace that grazes our knees. So, please
pass the suspension of task and venture, lend me your immortal
eyes, and pour me the wine, rosy and bright as your cheeks.

GASPARILLA

Hundreds of red Solo cups line the streets; from a distance,
they look like a long, broken string of plastic rubies.

If I come close enough to pick one up and listen,
I can hear the ocean of promises that surged last night,
see the stains from the lips that opened for them.

When I'm really quiet, I can make out the trace
of a breathless moan so familiar I could easily mistake it
for my own, until the chorus begins to rise at my feet.

And I imagine this one to be a child's birthday hat;
that one, a bell that once rang for every crawling thing
as it was given a name. The one in my hand is a shell
that was once a home.

I hold it gently, remembering myself among the long string
of broken hearts abandoned on the roadside, desperate
to beat myself alive, to reshape into something with wings,
to throw off the heavy rags and dine with the king.

MAKE ME FLOWERS

Compel my feet to venture far and wide,
Beyond the familiar paths so painless;
To risk the sunless way where sorrows hide
Beneath the shame that shadows loveliness;
To go where eyes flicker in caverns deep,
Their radiance dimmed by perpetual choices
To pause the pain through long and dreamless sleep
And shut the ears to the warning voices.
I remember how brightly his eyes shined
When childhood's endless suns lit them in gold.
And now he's made a prison for his mind,
But maybe he would take my hand to hold?
O, Love, as I pursue him, be my guide.
Take me gently; make me flowers by his side.

A FRACTION

I know I've reached the point of hugging you too long,
too fiercely, as if you've just returned home from war.

I realize it's the embrace of a body taking an imprint,
a mind bent on remembering your arms, your voice,
your scent, your soul.

What do these arms think they can offer? A shelter?
A vault? A love you can live inside?

No, flesh and bone can't save you, but I wonder if it's possible
for you to know a fraction of your worth by how much

I don't want to let go.

BACK INTO THE CAVE

Your soul is the color of the sea
in the morning—like your eyes—
and has a quiet beauty, like a pearl
of dew on a blade of grass.

But your god is in your belly again,
your hands are full of offerings,
and the only peace in your voice
is in my memory.

PLUMERIA

The day after he died was Mother's Day.
I awoke to a pillow soaked by a flood of timelines
retraced, conversations replayed, possibilities
destroyed—his voice apologizing in my head.

I left at dawn; my legs carried my shattered heart
around the neighborhoods, sunglasses masking
my swollen eyes. I must've looked crazy, my gaze fixed
intently on the sky as if it were a book of answers
written in a language I could not read.

Sorrow has a way of thinning the veil. I stopped
for every small wonder, each leaf and blossom,
caught every note dropping from the sparrow's throat.

I came to a plumeria tree with blooms like the breast
of my childhood bird, a hopeful mix of yellow and white.
Stepping onto a manicured lawn, I bent the branch toward me
so that I could breathe the beauty, but then it cracked,
and the whole tip of the plant suddenly became stolen property
in my hands. Right at that moment, the blinds in the window

moved, and I waved as if to say, "I'm sorry, I never meant
for this to happen." But they snapped closed.

I set the branch down, carefully, as if I was visiting
a gravesite, and backed away to prove I wanted nothing—
except a different ending to his story.

I wish they could've seen the moment before the break,
the way their flower fulfilled its priestly purpose,
offering incense for prayer. I wish they could've been close
enough to see the spiral of petals blazing against the darkness
like the northern lights over the world on the night he died,
to comprehend the desperate need the flower could not meet
and the way it whispered to me of the One who could.

WHEN I SEE YOU AGAIN

With the hem of your pants singed,
the edges of your shirt frayed by fire,
ash and soot clinging to your shoes,
a smile I have only dreamed of
will spread across your face—

warmer than the summer afternoons we spent
in the backyard trees pretending we were raised
by wolves, brighter than the splashes of laughter
painted on the ceiling as we rolled down
the slide we'd made of your bed,
sweeter than your kind and gentle soul.

You will be more yourself
than I ever knew you to be here,
His mercy dripping its honey
over your wounds.

And there will be no fear in our embrace.

A HIDING PLACE

You could hide here on my land,
inside my walls,
under my family name.

You could hide inside my voice,
beside my marching feet,
behind my posts.

I have hidden your tears in mine,
your hurt inside my chest,
your land on my soil.

For a long time, Jewish blood
was hidden from my story;
maybe I've been hiding it, too,
by believing it was not enough to burn.
Even if it was none, it would be enough
to hide you in my veins.

I will hide you in my prayers,
take your language to my lips,
sow love for you into the hearts
of my four children.
I will cherish my resurrected name,
Galit, and craft my waves of words.

Your tears will be my tears
and your joy will be my joy
and your future will be my future.
What is an oath but a promise
not to hide when needed most?

FOR PEACE

Peace slept soundly on her mother's breast.

She danced wildly, the sunrise flaming in her eyes.

She told a story to the grandchildren gathered at her feet.

She rose early to sing the Sh'ma with a father and his son.

She waited in the date cookies shaped like Torah scrolls
for the children to finish their dreams.

And then Peace was ripped from her mother's breast—
burned, bled, desecrated and dragged down to Sheol
into an endless tunnel of grief.

Night has devoured everything but the flicker we hold,
trembling,

as the brave fight with the hearts of lions and the help of angels
to bring her home.

TREASURE

On our first girl's trip to the mall,
she picked out a cheap starfish necklace
and asked me to buy it for her friend
who was moving away. It felt flimsy
in my hands, but her eyes were round
and genuine as rare coins.

I said, "You know it's not real gold,
so it might tarnish or break more easily."
She laid her hand over the once golden
chain around her neck—the one she never
takes off—and said, "Well, she gave me
this rusty old thing, but I cherish it
like it's gold."

With a little bag swinging by her side,
the tarnished token from a true friend
hanging near her heart, she walked
a step ahead of me, across silk-white tiles
gleaming as the sun poured through
the skylights.

A TORCH

The fate
of an empty
cookie tin
shaped
like a pillar
is decided
in one short
pause.
My cluttered
counters long
to be free of it,
but look how it
curves!

The deep hollow
invites me
to turn it over
in my mind,
lift it to the light,
observe the allure
of a shadowy trench
enclosed by satiny
silver, and in a blink
it is understood:
the full truth of it

is not yet known.

I set it down
and walk away,
leaving it
to glow.

A beat later, he enters.
I wait out of sight,
like someone
who has set out a gift.

He stops.
In one short
pause, he apprehends
telescope or burrow
or drum or black hole
or tunnel of doom,
and in a blink
he's sprinting,
the tin held high
as a torch, yelling
to his sister,
"Let's play puppies!"

FRUIT OF THE VINE

Rain batters the ground in a barrage of beats,
knocking on thirsty soil, and the roots

open gracefully to the cool, bare offering.
The cadence slows. A breeze murmurs

through pearl-studded green. Reaching down
like father's arms, sunbeams gift golden nectar

to the lips of leaves, and sugar is made, secretly,
from light. Sap courses up the vine, coaxing buds

into blossoms that will burst into fruit and drop
harmony into the harvester's hands.

The Vinedresser will crush, ferment, refine, mature.
And prune the fruitful vines. Finally, He will present

the vintage at a feast where the world-weary gather
and pour them a cup of you growing in Him.

EVE

She pressed it to her lips,
exploring the skin with her tongue:
smooth as a river stone,
cool as morning.

She bit down.

Eyes wide as worm moons,
she hurried to share,
but something entirely foreign
passed through:
a tangy prick of rot.

Her tongue ablaze,
she spat out the pulp,
but the juice slithered down,
cleaving near her voice box,
sticking like ash to her chin.

She tried to swallow,
but the sensation
was too painful—
as if Earth itself
had become lodged
in her throat.

The ground pulled heavily
on her bones.
She had never been so aware
of her skin, the way it clung
too tightly; had never known
the horrifying sensation
of wanting to slink out of it.

Her cheeks ignited, apple red.
Her heart thrashed against the bars
of its cage; the stomach now ruled
in its place.

The sky drained of color,
pomegranates bled,
goldfinches fell quiet.
The texture of grass, bark,
the delicate filament of leaves—
all of it flattened on a page.

The breeze carried no whispers;
the music of the river quieted;
sunlight swarmed like bees.

She coiled her arms tightly
around her bare flesh.
The pit in her stomach
made it nearly impossible
to take in breath.
Her husband's face contorted;
hers was a gnarled shell.

Their eyes met.
They held an eternal silence
before dropping to their knees
to grope for a shield of leaves.

And then she heard footsteps,
soft as a prayer.

PUBLISHER'S NOTE

Alchemy of Praise is the inaugural poetry collection from poet Wendy Kieffer. As publishers, we are honored to present this compilation and to celebrate these beautiful contributions of art crafted through written word. Just as alchemy seeks to transform base metals into gold, Wendy transmutes the ordinary, allowing us to see it with fresh eyes. We pray this collection will widen your imagination and carry you further up, further in, and further out.

May these poems awaken something essential within you as you discover life and beauty in and through this *Alchemy of Praise*.

Warmest regards,

Zach Elliott

V3 Press

ACKNOWLEDGEMENTS

My deepest gratitude truly belongs to God who guides, comforts, sustains and inspires me. Thank You, Father, for all the ways you bring beauty from ashes.

To my husband, William, there aren't enough words to express how grateful I am for all you have given. You have seen these poems through every stage; thank you for always making your ears "ready." To my children, God's gorgeous poems, thank you for your patience during this process and for all the ways you inspire me. To my parents, thank you for a lifetime of encouragement, for eyes that always mirrored my worth.

A profound thanks to Zach and Cammie Elliott and the team at V3 for believing in me and for the beautiful ways you love and lead like Jesus. To my talented friend, Sarah Sisco, thank you for your stunning artwork—I can't imagine this collection without it. Thank you to Meg Ryan for your keen eyes and intuition and for the invaluable help with the fine-tuning. To Melody Farrell, thank you for your vision, for pulling it all together so artfully. To my *anam cara*, Michelle Aždajić, thank you for lending your discerning eyes to this project and for your love of beauty which nourishes me. Thanks also to my cherished friend Dejan Aždajić for your help with polishing. To Patricia Tiffany Morris, Jasmine Morgan, and Angela Johnson, thank you for your generous ears.

To my dear friends, Lance and Michelle Laytner, thank you for your trusted counsel and faithfulness. To Crystal Mitchell, thank you for walking through the fires by my side and for covering my needs in prayer. A deep thanks to Bruce and Debi Cohen for beautifully shaping my early years of faith. And a bottomless thank you to all the artists who have inspired me who are too many to name.

Finally, thank you reader, for holding these words in your hands.

"Before the night arrives – come, come all!
A unified effort, stubborn and lively
of a thousand arms. Can the stone be rolled
off the mouth of the well?"
~Rachel Bluwstein

REFERENCES

Section One excerpt from:

Mechthild of Magdeburg. "Effortlessly", from *For Lovers of God Everywhere: Poems of the Christian Mystics*, edited by Roger Housden. Hay House, 2009.

Section Two excerpt from:

Teasdale, Sara. "The Wind in the Hemlock", from *The Collected Poems of Sara Teasdale*. Buccaneer Books, 1996.

Section Three excerpt from:

Bluwstein, Rachel. "Expectation", from *Aftergrowth*, edited by Shachar Weis. Bettafish Books, 2020.

Acknowledgements excerpt from:

Bluwstein, Rachel. "Here on earth - not in the clouds, above", from *Aftergrowth*, edited by Shachar Weis. Bettafish Books, 2020.

LIFE + BEAUTY

The LAB Initiative cares for culture by identifying and investing in efforts that fuel the common good. Specifically, the LAB Initiative contributes financial resources each year to combat human trafficking through survivor care, demand reduction, enforcement, and early intervention efforts.

A portion of the proceeds from your purchase of Alchemy of Praise will go to support the LAB Initiative's efforts. We invite you to increase your gift with a direct contribution. Learn more about the LAB Initiative by scanning the QR code below:

ABOUT THE AUTHOR

Wendy Kieffer is passionate about truth and beauty and the One to whom they point. She is the Conservatory Poet for VUVIVO Ministries and cohosts the monthly poetry podcast featured on LAB the Podcast (Life + Beauty). After earning an English degree from the University of South Florida, she relocated to New York City to pursue the arts but found her calling when her faith in God was rekindled. Wendy now resides in Florida and is a mother of four, serving alongside her husband as a deacon, teacher, and worship leader within their congregation. *Alchemy of Praise* is her debut poetry collection.

www.WendyKieffer.com

Milton Keynes UK
Ingram Content Group UK Ltd.
UKHW050152180824
447047UK00020B/242